The Classroom Teacher's Behavior Management Toolbox

The Classroom Teacher's Behavior Management Toolbox

Roger Pierangelo
Long Island University

George Giuliani
Hofstra University

INFORMATION AGE PUBLISHING, INC.
Charlotte, NC • www.infoagepub.com

Library of Congress Cataloging-in-Publication Data

A CIP record for this book is available from the Library of Congress
http://www.loc.gov

ISBN: 978-1-68123-475-5 (Paperback)
         978-1-68123-476-2 (Hardcover)
         978-1-68123-477-9 (ebook)

Printed in the United States of America

Contents

SECTION **I**

Understanding High Risk Behavior

SECTION **II**

How Ego Functions Effect a Child's Behavior

SECTION **III**

Self-Esteem

SECTION **IV**

Management Tools

SECTION **V**

How to Help Students Feel Good About Themselves in Order to Reduce Inappropriate Behavior

SECTION **VI**

Final Word

Introduction

The *Classroom Teacher's Behavior Management Toolbox* focuses on practical and productive techniques that can be used in a variety of behavior crisis situations that may occur in a classroom. Teachers have told us that one of their major concerns has been dealing with severe behavior problems in the classroom and the fear of not knowing how to handle the various situations.

While there are many different types of crisis situations that may occur, having the proper "tools" can prevent a situation from becoming even worse. This book provides a variety of management tools for all types of situations. These tools have been gathered over the years and have been very successful in actual classroom situations.

SECTION I

Understanding High Risk Behavior

1

What is High Risk Behavior?

As a special or general education teacher you will come in contact with a variety of personality types in the classroom. For the most part, teachers are put on the firing line with little or no training in why children do what they do. They are expected to help children learn but are not trained in understanding the numerous dynamic obstacles that prevent children from reaching this objective. Most teachers have not taken courses on human nature and dynamics and are not aware of symptomatic behavior and what is means. This lack of understanding creates immense frustration which only hinders the teacher's progress in working with fostering children's academic success.

All teachers need to understand the inner workings of children who are experiencing trouble in school. Understanding what causes children to choose certain behavioral patterns can help reach them sooner and prevent long lasting scars.

This book will present you with an easy to understand basis of why children do what they do. It is our hope that this insight will allow you to work more effectively on the real issues that may be creating problems in and

The Classroom Teacher's Behavior Management Toolbox, pages 3–4
Copyright © 2016 by Information Age Publishing

3

outside of school. We have also provided step by step suggestions on what to do when a specific behavior occurs in your classroom. The suggestions are only guidelines on what to do. It is critical to understand that patterns of inappropriate behavior should always be shared with the school psychologist or child study team. We hope this book acts as reference tool for early identification of problems seen in everyday classrooms.

$$2$$

Symptoms Versus Problems

Dynamic or internal problems (i.e., conflicts, fears, insecurities), create tension. The more serious the problem, the greater the level of tension experienced by a child. When tension is present, behavior is used to relieve the tension. The more serious the problem/s the greater the tension and the behavior required to relieve this tension becomes more immediate. As a result, the behavior may be inappropriate and impulsive rather than well thought out.

When tension is very high it may require a variety of behaviors to relive the dynamic stress. These behaviors then become symptoms of the seriousness of the problem. That is why the frequency and intensity of the symptomatic behavior reflects the seriousness of the underlying problems.

As the child becomes more confident or learns to work out his problems (i.e., through therapy), the underlying problems become smaller. As a result, they generate less tension and consequently less inappropriate, impulsive or self-destructive behavior patterns.

The Classroom Teacher's Behavior Management Toolbox, pages 5–6
Copyright © 2016 by Information Age Publishing

If a child does not recognize or does not have the label for the problem then the tension is usually released through some form of behavior. We call these outlets of tension behavioral symptoms. These behavioral symptoms are sometimes misidentified as problems and therefore treated as such. When this occurs the problem only gets worse. If one sees a fever as the problem, then treating that alone will exacerbate the problem. These behavioral symptoms become the first signal noticed by teachers, parents, and professionals.

Therefore, it is very important for teachers to understand the difference between symptoms and problems. If this is not fully understood, a great deal of frustration will occur in trying to extinguish the symptom on both the part of the child and the teacher.

The identification of symptoms as an indication of something more serious is another first step in helping children work out their problem.

$$3$$

Examples of Symptomatic Behavior

Examples of typical symptomatic behavior patterns that may be indicative of more serious concerns may include those shown in Figure 3.1.

While many of these symptoms may indicate the presence of a problem, several guidelines can be used to determine the seriousness of the problems.

1. Consider how often the symptoms occur. The more serious the problem the greater amount of tension generated. The greater amount of tension the more frequent will be the need to release this tension. Therefore, the greater the frequency of the symptom, the greater chance that the problem/s are serious.
2. Consider how long the symptoms last. The more serious the problem the greater the degree of tension generated. The greater the degree the longer it will take to release the tension. Therefore, the longer the duration of the symptoms the more serious the problem

The Classroom Teacher's Behavior Management Toolbox, pages 7–8

Impulsivity	Lies constantly
frequently hands in incomplete work	Awkward
gives many excuses for inappropriate behavior	fearful of adults
constantly blames others for problems	fearful of new situations
panics easily	verbally hesitant
Distractible	Hypoactive
short attention span	Hyperactive
over-reactive	fears criticism
physical with others	rarely takes chances
Intrusive	moody
unable to focus on task	defies authority
Procrastinates	anxious
Squints	not able to generalize
turns head while listening	insecure
Disorganization	trouble starting work
Inflexibility	tires easily
Irresponsibility	controlling
poor judgment	overly critical
Denial	forgetfulness
Daydreaming	painfully shy
unwillingness to venture a guess	overly social
unwillingness to reason	slow starter
social withdrawal	argumentative
constant use of self-criticism	destroys property
bullies other children	lazy
needs constant reassurance	inconsistency
poor reader	poor spelling
Argumentative	

Figure 3.1

3. Consider how serious the reactions are at the time of occurrence. The more serious the problem the more intense the level of tension coming off the problem will be.

4

Energy Drain and its Effect on Behavior and Learning

Individuals With Low Levels of Tension and Stress

Everyone possesses a certain amount of psychic energy to use in dealing with the everyday demands and stresses of life. In normal development there is a certain amount of stress but because of an absence of major conflicts which tend to drain energy, the individual has more than enough to keep things in perspective. Consequently, the division of energy usually results in what we call positive behavior symptoms.

For instance, in school the child, will exhibit (more often than not) behaviors that include, good concentration, responsibility with school work, consistency, age appropriate attention span, flexibility, appropriate memory, high frustration tolerance, appropriate peer interaction, organization and an appropriate ability to focus on tasks. One will hear these comments from teachers and notice many at home when the child is involved with homework. It is also important that it is kept in mind that not every child who is conflict free will exhibit these symptoms all the time. Only become concerned if patterns of behaviors reflect a potential problem.

The Classroom Teacher's Behavior Management Toolbox, pages 9–11
Copyright © 2016 by Information Age Publishing

If the child is conflict free, one will also notice certain positive behavior patterns at home. These will include (more often than not), normal strivings for parental approval, resiliency, willingness to reason, willingness to try, appropriate judgment and normal responses to discipline. Again keep in mind that these patterns may vary to some degree during adolescence and still be within "normal" limits.

If the child is not experiencing any major problems, he/she will usually have little difficulty falling asleep. While they may have problems waking up, as many of us do, it will not interfere in their ability to get to school. A problem like this is only serious when it affects one's ability to function, usually referred to as a functional impairment. Such would be the case if a child could not get up every morning and was consistently late to school. This type of symptomatic behavior might be a signal of a more serious problem.

Socially, the child will (more often than not) maintain social interactions; show a willingness to try new social experiences and treat his/her peers appropriately.

Individuals With High Levels of Tension and Stress

However, when serious conflicts arise, the available energy must be "drained away" to deal with the conflicts like white blood cells to an infection. Since energy must be drained away there is less available energy to keep things in perspective.

When a parent or teacher observes a pattern of behaviors similar to these, he/she should automatically become aware that some serious problem may exist. These symptoms are not the problems but an outgrowth of a serious problem. It is therefore very important for the parent to try to identify what the problem or problems are so that treatment can take place.

If it is suspected that some difficulty exists, one should not hesitate initiating a referral or consultation with the school psychologist or contact a local therapist for a consultation. Like an "infection," waiting too long will only aggravate the situation.

Consequently, when such serious problems or conflicts arise, they will drain off energy normally used for home and school. As this energy is drained away to deal with these serious issues, negative symptomatic behavior patterns will develop. Such symptoms should indicate to you that a problem exists and needs to be defined as soon as possible. These negative behavior patterns, indicating the presence of conflict/s will be observed in many areas of the child's life.

For instance, at school the child may now exhibit negative symptoms like inability to focus on task, procrastination, disorganization, denial, irresponsibility, inflexibility, projecting the reasons for problems on everyone and everything else, selected forgetting, daydreaming and so on. At home a parent may observe oversensitivity, over-reactions, forgetfulness, unwillingness to venture out, unwillingness to reason, stubbornness, lying, exaggeration and possible somatic complaints such as stomach aches, headaches and so on. You may even begin to notice changes in the child's sleeping patterns. He/she may have great difficulty falling asleep since tension interferes with relaxation and may even begin sleep walking or showing other signs of restless sleep. In the morning you may find extreme resistance in getting up which may result in lateness or absence. More frequent nightmares may also be a signal of some unresolved inner conflicts.

Socially, one may observe the child withdrawing from social situations, constantly finding fault with peers, being unwilling to try new social experiences, expressing social fears or beliefs that no one likes him/her and so on.

Remember, that such symptoms only occur as a result of a deeper undefined problem. Once the problem is identified and resolved, the negative symptomatic behavior will dissipate since the tension will be alleviated. If caught early, most of these issues can be resolved in a relatively quick period of time. However, also be aware that even though the problem may be identified, many months or years may have passed and will result in a longer treatment period.

If therapy is required be aware that it can be a long term process, especially if the problems have been around for a long period of time. However, you can tell if your child is making progress in therapy by the reduction of the negative symptomatic behavior patterns. As a child begins to verbalize the issues and find better ways of coping, the tension becomes diminished. As the tension is reduced, the need for symptomatic behavior is also reduced. Therefore, a reduction in the frequency, duration, and intensity of negative symptoms will mean that the child is getting stronger and may be on the right track.

5

How a Healthy Ego Functions

When we think of an ego we think about the psychic system that filters the rules of society, social rules, awareness of our surroundings, appropriate reactions and behavior to situations, appropriate emotional reactions to situations, and so may more functions that come into play hundreds of times a day.

A healthy ego should be seen like a strong fort with very thick walls that can keep things out until the appropriate decisions on what to do can be determined. Imagine that in this fort lives an "ego team" of people who always try to operate on logic, common sense, intellect, and farness. Further, the ego team is responsible to filter and respond to things coming or being thrown at the fort every day. Because it is a healthy ego and has strong walls, the ego team can take their time in determining several factors for the best response such as:

- What exactly is being presented?
- What are all the facts or issues that need to be considered?
- What are the optional responses?

The Classroom Teacher's Behavior Management Toolbox, pages 15–16

15

- How will the options affect others?
- What do we know about the people involved in this situation?
- What are the consequences of the responses?
- What are the possible outcomes?

Since the ego team has time to consider all these factors the chances of a positive response and positive outcome increase dramatically. This is made possible by the lack of tension and stress they are under because of the strong walls of the fort. Being under such little stress allows them to take their time and consider everything. Consequently, the appropriate response to a situation will raise the ego team's confidence in their decision making ability. Further, the ego team's reputation among all the inhabitants of the fort becomes stronger because they see how logical and fair the responses are that are being made by the team every day. This commanded respect (respect gathered by the observation of good judgment) further enhances how the team feels about itself. With every added positive response the team grows in confidence and even if they should make a mistake, they have no trouble fixing or apologizing since that would be the logical common sense thing to do. A healthy ego always tries to work on common sense and logic and any response resulting from this will not confuse the ego. This is not the case in the fragile ego.

However, this does not mean that he/she will not make mistakes but their ability to bounce back is greater. Examples of behaviors you will observe when dealing with a child with a healthy ego include:

- Willingness to reason
- Takes responsibilities for actions
- Understands consequences
- Is aware of how his/her behavior affects others
- Able to apologize appropriately
- Able to delay impulses
- Asks for advice
- Reactions appropriate for issue at hand
- Not afraid to question
- Does not get defensive when getting advice

6

How a Fragile Ego Functions

L et's take that same analogy about a fort used in the concept of a healthy ego and what we see with a fragile ego is also a fort. However this fort is decayed with many portions missing or filled with large holes which do not provide the inhabitants or its ego team a clear sense of safety. When things are thrown at the fort they come right in without any protection or time to consider all the factors required for an appropriate response. Unlike the healthy ego where the ego team has time to consider many factors, the ego team in an unhealthy ego must respond immediately since its sense of vulnerability and fear is so much greater. Consequently, the actions taken are not well thought out and impulsive at best. As a result, the responses to these actions are problematic and the inhabitants of the fort are not confident in the ego team's ability to take care of them. This lack of confidence makes the ego team try to compensate to get back some respect but because of their inability to delay or consider all the factors, their responses get worse and have far greater negative consequences. When things come into the fort through the holes they must act quickly usually using a deflection method which means that they throw it back out quickly without awareness

The Classroom Teacher's Behavior Management Toolbox, pages 17–18
Copyright © 2016 by Information Age Publishing
17

of what they are dealing with or the consequences of this action. The main purpose is to rid the fort even if it is something that may actually be good for the fort. This may occur frequently because of the lack of energy available to the ego team to discriminate good from bad, dangerous from safe, mild from severe, minimal from harsh, etc. What you will observe from a student with an unhealthy ego follows:

- Procrastination
- Impulsivity
- Aggressiveness
- Verbal abuse
- Physically aggressive
- Lying
- Stealing
- Fabrication
- Rationalization
- Denial
- Projection on to others for their own behavior
- Not taking responsibility for their actions

$$7$$

Know Your Audience

One of the best tools you can learn as a teacher is to "know your audience." What this means is you will need to understand that what you see is often driven by motives you cannot see, and the techniques you use may need to focus on motive, rather than behavior, in order to help a student succeed. Sometimes students feel insecure, inadequate, frightened, overwhelmed, anxious, confused, etc. All of these emotions are usually very hard for children to express, so they may get insulated by withdrawal, anger, or acting out behavior. Knowing your audience is taking the time to learn about your students' fears and inadequacies and understand that they may need reassurance, not discipline, guidance, not punishment, further explanation or examples, not time outs, etc. However, no inappropriate behavior should be condoned and the tools in this book will teach you how to deal with those behaviors on one level. But on another level, a student may feel inadequate many times during the day and the tension from this may come out in the form of acting out or inappropriate behavior. Understanding your audience means that you realize that all behavior has a trigger and it is your responsibility to find that trigger (e.g., insecurity, anxiety, or panic

The Classroom Teacher's Behavior Management Toolbox, pages 19–20
Copyright © 2016 by Information Age Publishing
19

to name a few). When you see evidence of fragile ego functioning, you will need to take precautions with a student in two very important ways: (1) making sure that assignments are constructed to ensure a sense of completion; and (2) sense of success. The practical tools in Section VI: How to Help Students Feel Good about Themselves in Order to Reduce Inappropriate Behavior will assist you in accomplishing this for your students.

Knowing your audience also means that you look past behavior rather than react to it. You learn to figure out why your students do what they do. Remember, no student wants to fail and many students may communicate their state of mind, fears, and conflicts through behavior. Once you know what the behavior means, finding answers will make the student feel safer and more in control. Once you learn the real emotions behind behavior, you should develop an emotional dictionary so that the student can communicate his or her feelings verbally rather than act them out behaviorally.

Be aware that reactions may be due to a task being too difficult and causing him/her to deflect the inadequacy and fear of failure in some inappropriate behavioral fashion. In this case, knowing that all behavior has a trigger look back to possible conditions that may have led up to the reaction. Understanding a student's insecurities, fears, anxieties, and so forth, will help short circuit inappropriate reactions.

SECTION III

Self-Esteem

8

What Is Self-Esteem?

Self-esteem is feeling good about yourself. Because it is a feeling, self-esteem is expressed in the way that people behave. However, success is important for the growth of positive feelings about oneself. High self-esteem will allow your students to keep failure situations in proper perspective. Whether or not a failure situation is perceived as a learning experience, or as a self-punishment, depends on one's level of self-esteem.

Children as well as adults will vary in the type of self-esteem exhibited. We all feel more confident on some days than others. Feeling low self-esteem from time to time is not a problem. However, a pattern of low self-esteem should be observed in order for there to be a concern. Teachers can easily observe children's self-esteem by seeing what they do and how they accomplish it.

9

Understanding the Foundations of Self-Esteem

A Child With High Self-Esteem Will:

- feel capable of influencing other's opinions or behaviors in a positive way
- be able to communicate feelings and emotions in a variety of situations
- behave independently
- approach new situations in a positive manner
- exhibit a high level of frustration tolerance
- take on and assume responsibility
- keep situations in proper perspective
- communicate positive feelings about him/her
- be willing to try a new situation without major resistance

Such children will possess an internal locus of control. Consequently, they feel whatever happens to them is a direct result of their own behavior or actions. These children will therefore feel a sense of power over their environment.

The Classroom Teacher's Behavior Management Toolbox, pages 25–26

Children With Low Self-Esteem Will:

- communicate self-derogatory statements
- exhibit a low frustration tolerance
- become easily defensive
- listen to other's judgment rather than his/her own
- be resistant to new situations and experiences
- constantly blame others for their failures and problems
- have very little feeling of power and control
- lose perspective easily—(blow things out of proportion)
- avoid any situation that creates tension
- be unwilling to reason

Such children will possess an external locus of control. Consequently, these children feel that whatever happens to them is the result of fate, luck, or chance.

In order to fully understand self-esteem, one must consider the factors involved. Self-esteem occurs when children experience the positive feelings of satisfaction associated with feeling:

Connected—A child feels good relating to people, places, and things that are important to her and these relationships are approved and respected by others.

Unique—A child acknowledges and respects the personal characteristics that make him special and different, and receives approval and respect from others for those characteristics.

Powerful—A child uses the skills, resources, and opportunities that she has in order to influence the circumstances of her own life in important ways.

10

Practical Suggestions to Improve Self-Esteem

The following suggestions are offered to enhance children's positive feelings about themselves. These recommendations require consistency, genuineness, and discrimination on the part of teachers and parents. No one suggestion by itself will have long lasting effects. A combination of techniques will have greater impact. However, you should always keep in mind that many other factors, not within your control (i.e., peer group, school environmental factors, perception etc.), will also contribute to children's self-esteem. However, the roles of teachers and parents are crucial and can offset a child's difficulties in other areas.

Be Solution Oriented

An important step in building your students' self-esteem is to teach solutions rather than blame. Some children are very "blame oriented". When something goes wrong, he/she is quick to "point the finger" at someone else. Children who are blame oriented not only become easily frustrated, but never learn how to handle obstacles. Teaching your students solutions begins with simple statements like, "Who's at fault is not important. The

The Classroom Teacher's Behavior Management Toolbox, pages 27–30

more important question is what we can do so that it doesn't happen again." Being solution oriented allows children a sense of control and resiliency when confronted with situations that could be ego deflating and lower their self-esteem.

Allow Children the Right to Make Decisions

While the statement, "No one promised them a democracy" may hold true in some situations, allowing your students the right to make decisions that affects their daily life can only enhance their self-esteem. Decisions about decorating lockers, seating arrangements, and free-time activities, and so forth, can make children feel some sense of control in what happens to them. Coupled with solution orientation, mistakes can be used as a positive learning experience. A good technique to use here is a forced choice technique. Provide the student with three options, all of which are acceptable to you, and ask them to choose which one they prefer. The student will feel like they are making the decision but all of the choices will lead to resolution and success.

Offer Alternative Ways When Handling a Situation

Some people know only one or two alternatives in handling situations. After these fail, frustration occurs. Conditioning your students to see many alternative ways of handling a situation or obstacle can also enhance their self-esteem. Asking children what they have tried and offering those options to other possible solutions, increases their "tool box." The more "tools" we have at our disposal, the easier life becomes. Individuals with limited "tools" tend to use avoidance and flight as a means of coping with frustration.

Teach Children the Proper Labels When Communicating Feelings

The ability to correctly label one's feelings is a factor in self-esteem. Children have a very difficult time communicating because they lack the proper labels for their feelings. When children are unable to label an internal feeling, it becomes trapped and the frustration may become manifested in behavior problems, physical symptoms and so on. When such feelings are manifested in other forms, they are usually misunderstood or misinterpreted. Teachers can offer children the correct labels. For example, you may want to say, "While the feeling you are expressing sounds like anger, it is really frustration and frustration is . . . Now that you know this, is there anything that is causing you frustration?"

Building an emotional vocabulary allows communication to flow more easily and reduces a child's unwillingness to deal with situations.

Allow Children the Opportunity to Repeat Successful Experiences

Whenever possible, allow your students the chance to handle any job or responsibility in which they have proven success. A foundation of positive experiences is necessary for self-esteem. Since the child has mastered skills required for the job, any opportunity to repeat success can only be ego inflating. Jobs such as collecting homework from other students, handing out materials, cleaning the room, are examples of repetitive experiences that will lead to a feeling of consistent success. However, in the cases of children with severe disabilities, the activities chosen will have to take into consideration the limitations so as not to frustrate them.

Allow Avenues for Disagreement

Children with higher self-esteem will always feel they have an avenue to communicate their concerns. Even though the result may not go in their favor, the knowledge that a situation or disagreement can be discussed allows the child to feel some involvement in his destiny. This factor becomes important when one sees that many children with low self-esteem feel a loss of power in affecting change.

Help Your Students Set Realistic Goals

This is a very crucial issue in helping children improve their self-esteem. Some children will set unrealistic goals, fall short, and feel like a failure. Repeated over a period of time, these unrealistic goals will result in consistent failure leading to more unrealistic goals. This circular behavior sometimes results with children becoming unwilling to venture out or take chances. The more limited children become in their experiences, the less chance for success. Avoidance, passivity, rejection of an idea or experience will only reinforce feelings of inadequacy.

Help your students by defining their objective. You may want to ask them what they want to accomplish. After this, try to help them define the steps necessary to accomplish the task and break down the task into smaller, controllable tasks that have the greatest chance of success. Each step becomes a goal in itself. Children should not see one final goal, but a series of smaller goals leading to a final point. In this way they will feel accomplishment at every step.

Use a Reward System to Shape Positive Behavior

Punishment tells a child what not to do, while rewards inform them of what to do. Rewarding positive behavior increases self-esteem. Children enjoy winning the approval of teachers, parents, and peers, especially when it comes to a job or task. You may want to use rewards such as notes indicating how proud you feel about what the child has accomplished. Rewards can also be special time where the student can choose from a list of fun activities, lunch with the teacher etc.

Make Sure You Communicate to Parents Not to Pave Children's Roads

Some parents make the mistake of reducing frustration for children to the point where the child receives a distorted view of the world. Children with high self-esteem get frustrated. However, they tend to be more resilient because they have previously handled frustrating situations and worked out the solutions themselves. When parents rush to the aide of their children, finish assignments for them, or make excuses, they are changing the environment to prevent them from becoming frustrated. However, they are unwittingly reinforcing children's low self-esteem and creating feelings of learned helplessness. After a while, children become dependent upon their parents to "bail them out" when they are confronted with frustration. The need to master the environment and find solutions to challenges is crucial to positive self-esteem. The old saying, "Catch me a fish and I'll eat today, teach me to fish and I'll eat forever," seems to apply.

In conclusion, improving your students' self-esteem is a process that needs to be viewed in a positive way. Altering feelings of low self-esteem offers children a more positive future.

11

Understand Avoidance Behavior Patterns as an Indication of Low Levels of Confidence

Some of the first signs that a child is experiencing problems with learning are avoidance behaviors. These are techniques used by children to avoid what they perceive as a failure provoking or an ego-deflating situation. Children will often exhibit these symptoms at home and at school to avoid loss of parental approval, peer humiliation, or failure. They are avoiding:

- showing their parents they are not capable
- dealing with possible parental anger and frustration
- coming face to face with their own inadequacy
- dealing with peer pressure and possible ridicule

Some of the more common avoidance behaviors are discussed in detail below:

The Classroom Teacher's Behavior Management Toolbox, pages 31–33
Copyright © 2016 by Information Age Publishing
31

- **Selective forgetting**—If a child knows the batting averages of all baseball players, the words from most songs on the radio, the times of most TV shows, but habitually "forgets" to bring home his or her math book the child is exhibiting selective forgetting. The selectivity of the forgetfulness usually centers on areas of learning that the child may find frustrating.
- **Forgetting to write down assignments day after day**—This symptom may continue even after repeated requests or threats. The child exhibiting this symptom is most likely trying to avoid a perceived-failure experience.
- **Taking hours to complete homework classwork**—In this avoidance pattern the child seems to labor or procrastinates over school-work. Frequent trips to the kitchen for food, or to the bathroom, or to get a drink, or to sharpen a pencil, delay the possibility of what the child perceives will be failure. This symptom also occurs if a child is under tension and having difficulty concentrating for long periods of time.
- **Finishing homework or classwork very quickly**—The child exhibiting this symptom is trying to get the ego threatening situation (homework/classwork) over as quickly as possible. The child makes every attempt to "rush" through the assignments with little if any care or patience. Getting it over as quickly as possible almost makes it seem as if it never existed.
- **Not being able to get started with homework or classwork**—When a child's anxiety level is very high it is very difficult to "start the engine." He or she may spend a great deal of time getting ready for homework by arranging books, sharpening pencils, getting the paper out, opening the textbooks, getting a glass of water, going to the bathroom, and so on. Once again, the child is trying to avoid the task that he or she finds threatening.
- **Frequently bringing home unfinished classwork**—A child can exhibit this symptom for several reasons. One reason could be that the child has a low energy level and therefore has difficulty dealing with tasks involving sustained concentration. The second reason could be that the child is dependent upon parental assistance with homework. If the child's parents constantly sit next to the child when he or she is doing homework the child can become conditioned to their assistance and feel helpless without it. Since the child misses such support in the classroom, the child procrastinates in doing his classwork so that he or she can bring it home do it with his or her parents. The third reason could be the

child's need for attention. Bringing home unfinished classwork may necessitate a parent's sitting with him or her to complete the work. The child may see the parent as a "captive audience" and stop working or complain that he or she can't do the work if the parent tries to leave. Bringing home unfinished classwork extends the period of attention the child receives from his or her parents; however, these situations usually become more tense and negative as the hours progress and the parent's patience waivers.

▪ **Consistently leaving long term assignments until the last minute** Avoidance of school related tasks, especially long-term ones, is a frequent symptom of children with low energy levels. The behavior is analogous to avoiding paying a big bill when one has very little money. Another way one can avoid paying a bill is to forget that the bill exists. Similarly, children who are anxious about being able to complete an assignment successfully try "magical thinking"; they try to wish the assignment out of existence or believe that it will magically be finished without any participation on their part.

▪ **Complaining of headaches, stomachaches, etc., before or after school**—A child's very high tension levels over an extended period of time may result in somatic (bodily) complaints. These complaints, while real to the child, may indicate his or her avoidance of an uncomfortable or ego-deflating situation. The physical discomfort or ailment becomes the excuse for not performing well or not performing at all.

▪ **Exhibiting "spotlight" behaviors**—"Spotlight" behaviors are behaviors that focus attention on the child-calling out, laughing out loud, getting up out of seat, annoying other children. When a child "spotlights" it is usually a release of tension. Some children use "spotlight" behaviors to alleviate the tension of academic inadequacy and may even hope to get into trouble to leave the room. In this way they will not have to deal with possible academic failure. Another reason for "spotlight" behaviors is the need on the part of the child to be in control. However, the more controlling a child is, the more out of control that child may feel. The third reason for "spotlight" behaviors is to gain the teacher's attention. However, in this way the child is determining when he or she gets attention, not the teacher. It is better for the teacher to spontaneously and randomly pay attention to such a child when the child is not expecting it. In this way the teacher (or the parent) can reduce the child's impulsive need to seek attention.

12

Understand How Negative Energy Drains Confidence and Effects Behavior and Learning

If a child is experiencing many conflicts, problems, insecurities and so forth, there will be an increase in the number, types, and degree of negative symptoms the child exhibits. All conflicts require energy, therefore, the greater the frequency, duration, and intensity of the symptoms, the greater the energy drain on the child. The energy required to deal with these conflicts must come from somewhere, and it tends to come from constructive processes such as concentration, memory, attention and so on. Since these constructive processes—so necessary for success in school—become threatened the child will begin to suffer.

Everyone has a certain amount of psychic energy to use in dealing with the everyday stresses of life. In normal development there is a certain amount of stress, but, because of an absence of major conflicts that would tend to drain energy, the individual has more than enough energy to keep things in perspective.

The Classroom Teacher's Behavior Management Toolbox, pages 35–37
Copyright © 2016 by Information Age Publishing
35

The division of energy and the generally positive symptoms that result when a child is relatively "conflict free" may take on a certain pattern. As a result, the child will exhibit behaviors that include good concentration, responsibility with school work, consistency, age appropriate attention span, flexibility, appropriate memory, high frustration tolerance, appropriate peer interaction, organization, and an appropriate ability to focus on tasks. Parents will notice these behaviors at home when the child does homework and educators will notice it at school. Not every child who is conflict free will exhibit these symptoms all the time, but the child's habits and behaviors will be predominately positive and constructive.

The child will also exhibit positive behavior patterns at home. These will generally include normal strivings for parental approval, resiliency, and willingness to reason, willingness to try, exercising appropriate judgment, and responding normally to discipline. These patterns may vary to some degree during adolescence and still be within "normal" limits.

A relatively "conflict-free" child will usually have little difficulty falling asleep. While he or she may have problems waking up, as many of us do, it will not interfere in his or her ability to get to school. Socially, the child will generally maintain social interactions; show a willingness to try new social experiences and treat his/her peers appropriately.

When a child is troubled by serious conflicts his or her available energy must be "pulled" to deal with the conflicts, like white blood cells to an infection, and the child has less energy available to keep things in perspective. In this case the resulting symptoms and behaviors take on a different look.

Parents or educators, who suspect that a child is experiencing some difficulty because he or she exhibits some negative symptomatic pattern, do not hesitate to contact the school psychologist or contact a local therapist for a consultation. Following are examples of some of the causes of serious problems which might result in negative symptomatic behavior:

Intellectual Reasons
- Limited intelligence; slow learner
- Retardation

Social Reasons
- Peer pressure
- Peer rejection

Emotional Reasons
- Consistent school failure

- Traumatic emotional development
- Separation or divorce of parents
- High parental expectations
- Sibling performance
- Health-related problems
- Change in environment as a result of moving
- Abuse
- Dysfunctional family situation
- Parental loss of job
- Death in the family

Academic Reasons
- Learning disabilities
- Poor academic skills-math, reading
- Style of teacher incompatible with style of student
- Language difficulties
- Falling behind in school because of an imbalance in other areas (i.e., too social)

Negative behavior patterns such as those listed above will be evident in many areas of the child's life. For instance, at school the child may be unable to focus on task, may procrastinate, may daydream, may be disorganized, may reject help, may be irresponsible, inflexible, and selectively forgetful, and may project reasons for problems on everyone and everything else and so on. At home the child may be oversensitive, forgetful, reclusive, unreasonable, overactive, stubborn, untruthful, exaggerative, and may express somatic complaints such as stomachaches, headaches, and so on. The child's sleeping patterns may change. He or she may have great difficulty falling asleep since tension interferes with relaxation and may even begin to sleep walk or show other signs of restless sleep. The child may resist getting up in the morning which may result in lateness or absence. More frequent nightmares may also be a signal of some unresolved inner conflicts. Furthermore, the child may withdraw socially—constantly find fault with peers, be unwilling to try new social experiences, express social fears or express beliefs that no one likes him or her, and so on.

It is important to remember that such symptoms only occur as a result of a deeper undefined problem. Once the problem is identified and resolved and once the tension is alleviated, the negative symptomatic behavior will dissipate. If caught early, many such issues can be resolved in a relatively quick period of time. However, if the underlying problem is not identified for many months or years the treatment period will be longer.

SECTION IV

Management Tools

13

Behavior Crisis Management Tools

Pre-Empting Behavior

Purpose

This technique is a good "tool" to have when students are exhibiting certain inappropriate behaviors in a classroom and asking them to stop in front of the class has not worked.

Examples

Everyday certain students may exhibit behaviors that interfere in the performance, concentration or facilitation of learning for both the teacher and his/her peers. For instance, a student may continuously talk to another student, interfere with his/her work, disrupt lessons, call out, or bring the negative spotlight to him/herself in some manner. These negative, attention seeking behaviors will disrupt the flow of teaching and place you in a very difficult position.

The Classroom Teacher's Behavior Management Toolbox, pages 41–65
Copyright © 2016 by Information Age Publishing
41

What May Not Work

Many teachers will confront the student in front of the other students. This technique usually has very little success, especially with students who have more serious issues. This technique will actually offer the student more of a spotlight. Secondly, the student, who is already fragile, needs to save face in front of his peers so that there is a good chance he will talk back or become verbally resistant to your request.

Try This

The important issue here is to realize that a student who chooses this type of behavior pattern is actually very fragile and feels powerless. Confronting him/her in front of the audience provides him/her "power" that can prove to be a problem for both you and the student. You never want to allow yourself to be "caught" as you would be if you discipline this type of student in front of a crowd.

What we suggest is that you allow the class to enter the room and ask him/her to stay behind outside. Have the assistant cover the class while behind closed doors in the hallway you speak to the student. What you have now done is remove the audience and thereby removing a source of "power" for the student. The next thing is to set the boundary. Many teachers make the mistake by saying, "I want you to stop doing what you are doing..." If the child was able to stop it he would, but since we already know that he/she lacks internal controls saying it this way asks him to control his own behavior.

What you need to immediately establish is who is in charge. Therefore, you will need to say, "I can no longer allow you to interfere with John when he is working. I will no longer allow you to disrupt the class and my teaching". Then place the responsibility directly on the student by saying, "And if you choose to act inappropriately, I will take action to stop your behavior. Do you understand?"

If the student conforms to the boundary then you will need to reward him/her verbally or through some classroom experience so that you begin to shape his/her behavior. Remember reward tells a student what to do, punishment tells him what not to do.

Placing the responsibility for consequences on the part of the student by making him/her see that they are "Choosing to behave inappropriately" provides you with more power and control if they should continue their behavior.

Proximity Teaching

Purpose

The purpose of this tool is to establish a structure around a student who is unable to maintain control over his/her behavior.

Examples

Every day in classrooms across the country some student is unable to control his/her own behavior. As a result, he/she will present a problem for the classroom teacher when lessons are taking place. For instance, the student may tease or interfere in a student's work, may daydream, may be text messaging, may be making noises etc. For some students, this may be a pattern of behavior that they are unaware of since they lack self-monitoring skills. For others, it may be a release of tension, a lack of concentration, or the need to be the center of attention.

What May Not Work

For many students with internal control issues, what will not work in cases like this is setting boundaries from a distance through verbal directions. The greater the distance between the teacher and the student, the weaker the command and desired outcome will be. For students with internal control issues, asking them to stop from a distance is like asking running water from a faucet to shut itself off.

Try This

What you will need to do without skipping a beat is to work your way around the room while teaching until you are at the desk of the student who is having difficulty setting his/her own boundary. Placing your hand on his/her desk while teaching, will help in refocusing the student and center him/her back on the lesson. However, in cases where the student has a pattern of internal control issues, you will want to move him/her close to your desk so that when you move to proximity teaching you do not have far to go.

Use a Forced Choice Technique

Purpose

The purpose of this technique is to limit the behavior of students who try to negotiate everything.

Examples

There are times when the behaviors of certain students are exhibited by the need to negotiate everything you say or request. These students have difficulties internalizing boundaries and attempt to set boundaries of their own. This need usually stems from feeling out of control, since the more out of control a student feels, the more controlling he/she becomes. The need to control comes from vulnerability, anxiety or the fear of not knowing how to deal with things that are not predictable. Therefore, in the students' minds, these fears or anxieties can only be relieved if everything is predictable. However, the problem comes in because they feel that controlling everything will make things predictable and life does not always allow that to happen. Students with this behavior pattern will constantly say things like, "Why can't I?", or "Can I do this instead?" or "Don't I get a choice?"

What May Not Work

What usually does not work is giving in to the demands, requests or negotiations of controlling students when you have established what you need to be done. While these students can be very aggressive, convincing or assertive, they are still trying to control the environment. If you give in, you will be reinforcing the student's belief that they can control you and other things in his/her environment and as a result reinforcement will increase the frequency and intensity of such negotiation. You will then find yourself becoming very angry at the student who you will see as more powerful than you. However, keep in mind that it is not "Look what he is doing to me", but rather, "Look what I am allowing to happen."

Try This

We must be sensitive to the feelings that are present and motivate this need to control on the part of the student and try to direct it in a more positive manner. What we should use instead is what we call a forced choice technique. In this technique, the student who is trying to negotiate is offered two options, both of which are acceptable to you. It is sometimes preferable, especially if you know that a certain student has this pattern, to initiate the forced choice technique before he/she tries to negotiate. Choosing either one of your options will be fine, but the student feels he/she is making the decision. A forced choice technique basically says to the student, "You can do this or you can do that. Which one do you prefer?" or "You can do this before lunch or after lunch, which one do you prefer"? Again, the emphasis is on the forced choice. If the student says neither, then you say, "If you do not choose one of these, then I will choose for you, but I'd rather see you make the decision."

Learn What Triggers Certain Behaviors in Your Students: Finding Each Child's "Emotional Aura"

Purpose

The purpose of this technique is to learn how to prevent and short circuit potential outbursts and inappropriate behavior.

Examples

- John, an 11 year old student classified as a student with an emotional disturbance, strikes out at the boy sitting next to him without provocation.
- Mary, an eight year old girl with impulse control issues, quickly gets up out of her seat in the middle of a lesson and begins to walk around the room.
- Roberto, a 14 year old boy with behavior issues, begins to yell out and make fun of another student in the class.
- Zach, a six year old with emotional issues, gets frustrated and begins to destroy things on his desk.

Keep in mind that all of the above examples represent behaviors initiated by the students rather than reactive behaviors to someone else's behavior.

In all of these cases, the teacher first becomes aware of a problem at the time of the explosive outburst. However, these children exhibited a prior pattern of discomfort, tension or symptoms prior to the behavior which was not observed by anyone. For instance, if I am traveling in a car at 60 miles an hour and someone says, "Did you see that?" my first reaction will be, "No, we were traveling too fast." If we go five miles an hour, then I will see everything. Well, behavior often travels at 60 miles an hour, and as a result, we miss the signals given off by a student of an impending problem.

The symptoms exhibited prior to the emotional outburst are referred to as "emotional aura". For example, people with epilepsy will experience auras prior to the episodes which may allow them to pull over if they are driving, or take precautions not to hurt themselves when the episode occurs. While this aura may be a short period of time, it does provide an opportunity to do something that may prevent a more serious problem.

What May Not Work

What is often very frustrating for a teacher is disciplining the student for the same pattern of behavior with the student never seeming to incorporate the disciplines into self-control. While you may not be able to do anything on the first or second outburst ever observed, after that, you should have control over seeing what the trigger symptoms may be in order to step in before the outburst. What does not work is constantly disciplining the child after the behavior has occurred over and over and over. The child's lack of ability to use internal controls is evident by the consistent pattern of inappropriate behavior. Therefore, the better use of energy may be in prevention rather than crisis management.

Try This

After a student has exhibited a certain behavior pattern, have your aide or assistant closely observe him/her, recording all behaviors which may show discomfort, tension, or agitation to see which behaviors occur prior to the outburst. If for some reason you do not have an aide or assistant ask the school psychologist to come in and do a classroom observation to record the behaviors that precede the outburst (antecedent behaviors). Once these are recognized, you will have a prior indication of a potential problem. When you see these symptoms beginning (e.g., restlessness, daydreaming, head down on desk, scribbling etc.), take action immediately by either going over to the desk and using proximity teaching, or have your aide take him/her for a walk or errand. Short circuiting an inappropriate behavior and turning it into a positive experience will not only help you but offer the student a more positive outcome.

"This Is Not Open for Discussion"

Purpose

The purpose of this tool is to limit negotiation and control on the part of students when you need something done without question.

Examples

Students who have behavior issues will try and negotiate or control the environment since that offers them some predictability. Keep in mind that the more controlling a student is, the more out of control he/she actually feels so control reduces his/her anxiety. The problem is that at times he/she has a hard time relinquishing power and control to his/her teacher. This sometimes results in negotiation, opposition, defiance, and so on. All too often, these behavioral symptoms occur when a teacher is directing a class to do something and as a result the teacher gets into confrontation, threats, or disciplinary action in an attempt to get the students to conform. The problem here is that students with behavioral issues sometimes need a very small "canvas" or limited options in which to operate. The larger the "canvas" or the more options the greater the tension. This tension is what leads to the need to control.

What May Not Work

What does not work in this type of situation is not setting the rules beforehand when you definitely need the students to comply. Students with behavioral issues will always feel they can negotiate, sometimes not very appropriately, since they themselves lack boundaries or regard for authority.

Try This

If you are directing something that needs to be done, limit the opportunity for reaction by first saying: What I am about to tell you is something that needs to be done immediately. Therefore, it will not be open for discussion and I will not entertain any questions. I expect all of you to follow through on this requirement.

Controlling Student Outcomes: You Do and Then You Get

Purpose

The purposes of this technique is to control student outcomes and foster a sense of task completion and sense of accomplishment.

Examples

As a teacher, you will be confronted with many attempts by students with emotional issues to control their environment by wanting things their way. In many cases, these students will want their needs provided for first before they are willing to conform to your rules or requests. For instance:

- a student may promise that if you let him/her talk to a friend he/she will do the math class work, or
- if you let a student text message her friend she will do what you are asking, or
- if you just let them work on the computer they promise to do what you are asking after they finish

While these are just examples, many attempts at manipulating the environment are exhibited every day by these students and place the teacher in difficult positions.

What May Not Work

What definitely does not work is allowing a student who is trying to manipulate you or the environment to determine the rules governing completion of rules or tasks. Some students can be persistent in their attempts to get you to let them do it their way and eventually you may give in. However, this will only reinforce the student's beliefs that he/she can change your rule at any time.

Try This

The best rule for this type of situation is not to necessarily deny his/her request. After all, in some cases the request may be realistic and not unreasonable but doing it before the task is not acceptable. After all, this is very much like a child asking a parent for dessert before dinner but the parent lets them know they can still have the dessert but after dinner. So very calmly you tell the student, "You do this first, and then you get that." If the student comes up to you asking if he/she can now do what he/she wanted, you ask him/her, "Did you complete ..." If he/she says that he/she did not you simply say, "Well come back to me when you have completed it and we will talk." This technique allows the student to understand priorities and delay of gratification. The technique of "You do and then you get" is an effort saving approach when working with students who have issues of control.

Initiate a Vested Interest in the Student's Desire to Maintain Success

Purpose

The purpose of the tool is to help troubled students develop a sense of accomplishment and build an investment in being successful.

Example

Billy a student with emotional problems has never been successful in school because his issues prevent him from concentrating, focusing, attending to task, and completing assignments. His high levels of anxiety add to his perception that school is a waste and has no meaning for him. However, Billy's perception of school is based on his beliefs reinforced by his failure to succeed. With no investment or an identity that includes academic success, Billy will maintain the only identity he knows, a troubled, oppositional defiant young man.

What May Not Work

What does not work is exposing these troubled students to more and more work without first changing their negative perception of themselves and school. The only thing you will be doing here is to "build a house on water" and expect cooperation without first having a foundation of success.

Try This

Since success breeds success any child will welcome being validated in a positive way when it comes to school work. However, most troubled children have behaviors that prevent them from focusing and taking chances on doing academic work in which they have not been successful in the past. As a result, they rarely experience success in school and have nothing to lose since there is no investment or gains in their "success bank account." What is suggested is that you will need to initially present and use high success rate tasks to develop a sense of success, motivation, and control. The more consistent success a child has the less anxious they will be and therefore the more invested they will become in school. Try to put as many consecutive success rate tasks together (about 20–30) to begin changing the child's perception of him/herself and outlook on schoolwork.

High success rate tasks are adapted so that factors are added to increase the child's sense of accomplishment and positive experience. The use of changes in the following factors can greatly increase the rate of success necessary for a child to develop a vested interest in school:

1. Amount: Adapt the number of items that the learner is expected to learn or complete. *For example:* If student is to know the fifty states, have students only be responsible for remembering a certain number at a time. This would be dependent on the student's level of disability.

2. Length of Time Given for Assignment: Adapt the time allotted and allowed for learning, task completion, or testing. *For example:* Allow student additional time to complete timed assignments. However, if the total project is due by a particular time, have the student complete each portion of the project over various intervals with the required finished project due at a later time.

3. Level of Teacher Support: Increase the amount of personal assistance with a specific learner. *For example:* Allow for peer teaching. Pair the slower students with the more advanced students in order to provide support. Offer some sort of incentive to the more advanced student for assisting others. Design some type of contract with students that they could show to their parents indicating completion of their work and the assistance they are giving to others. Offer this as a bonus to their grades.

4. Types of Input: Adapt the way instruction is delivered to the learner. *For example:* Provide students with an audio and/or video tape of the lesson. Allow for field trips, guest speakers, peer teaching, computer support, video productions performed by students, incorporate lesson in other subjects areas.

5. Adjust Level of Difficulty: Adapt the skill level, problem type, or the rules on how the learner may approach the work. *For example:* Allow the student to be creative providing that task is completed according to instructor's specifications. For example the student may draw a picture of the assignment, do an interview, etc. depending on subject. Allow the student to come up with the idea. Accept any reasonable modifications.

6. Adapt Output Options: Adapt how the student can respond to instruction. *For example:* Allow students to draw pictures, write an essay, complete specific computer software program relating to lesson.

7. Level of Participation of Student: Adapt the extent to which a learner is actively involved in the task. *For example:* Tailor the stu-

dent's participation in a task to his or her abilities, whether intellectual or physical.

8. Alternate Materials: Adapt the goals or outcome expectations while using the same materials. *For example:* In a writing assignment, alter the expectations for a disabled student who takes longer to write a paragraph.

9. Substitute Curriculum: Provide different instruction and materials to meet a student's individual goals. *For example:* Instead of discussing the reasons for the civil war, have the disabled student work on a puzzle showing the Union and Confederate states.

Set Control Boundaries Several Times a Day

Purpose

The purpose of this tool is to establish behavioral boundaries with your students in a realistic manner several times a day.

Examples

Mrs. Jones' class is very excited to get into school in the morning and everyone runs in to get to his/her locker first. As a result everyone is pushing and teasing.

Mr. Williams' class can't wait to get to lunch and closely watch the clock for the bell to ring. Once that happens the class rushes out of the room to lunch. Mrs. Ortiz's class can't wait to get out of school and as a result they pack up and run to the door before she has a chance to speak with them.

Mr. Samuelson's class is "every one for him or herself" and never seems to be centered. His style is loose, and as a result, his class is unstructured and pretty much does what it wants without direction or plans.

What May Not Work

When working with children with special needs, one must always be aware of the number of students that do not possess internal controls and self-monitoring qualities. As a result, if left up to their own devices, they will often operate on impulse, self-serving behaviors, control and resistance to tasks. When a class is not focused or grounded, you will have 8, 10, 15 etc. students all operating on their own schedule or needs. What they need is a focus, a center, and a person in charge who leads the way and establishes boundaries.

Try This

Four times a day you will want to pull the class together in a group so that you can create a feeling of control and a central starting and ending place for the day. This procedure should occur at the beginning of the school day, before lunch, after lunch and before the end of the school day. These four boundary periods led by the teacher and the assistant will provide the necessary boundaries, priorities, structure, and leadership from which many students with special needs will benefit. During these group boundary meetings, you will want to lay out the morning routine, discuss what will be done after lunch, structure the afternoon, and provide guidance about what needs to be done or brought in for the next day and a brief overview of the next day's activities. This may also be a good time for handouts to parents, to go over homework required for the next day, and to provide a positive thought for the day.

Avoid Placing Yourself in a Position of a Judge

Purpose

The purpose of this issue of the Classroom Management Series is to provide guidelines when responding to an incident or altercation between two children that the teacher has not personally witnessed.

Examples

Mrs. Jones is busy marking papers when she hears the children yelling that two boys are fighting. Mrs. Jones goes over to the scene and calms everyone down. She then proceeds to ask the boys what happened and each blames the other. Mrs. Jones knows that one of the boys has a history of taunting the other students and acting aggressively so she tells him that this is the last straw and there will be consequences. The other boy, a passive child is told to return to his seat without consequence.

Mr. Eggers turns the corner and sees two of his students screaming at each other and pushing one another violently. He separates the two students and asks them what happened. Each blames the other and tries to convince the teacher that the other should be punished. The teacher is not sure who to believe so he continues to ask more questions in hopes of determining who is at fault.

What May Not Work

What does not work in any of these cases is gathering information from two unreliable, subjective, self-protective sources and trying to determine who may have started the altercation. Placing yourself in the position of being a judge in situations that you did not personally witness minimizes your authority and the respect your students will have for you. It is one thing to personally observe an altercation and see who started it. It is another to try to determine who is at fault when you were not there.

Try This

If you begin from the position that two students fighting have both chosen to use methods that are unacceptable, regardless of who started, then the only position is that both students need to suffer consequences for their choice of actions. After all, many other options may have existed (i.e., walking away, telling the teacher, talking it out, asking other students to help out etc.).

The students need to know that inappropriate actions regardless of motive have consequences. You should tell both students the following, "There is no way I can determine who started this and who is at fault since I did not directly see what happened. However, the fact that both of you chose to use actions that are not acceptable will result in consequences for both of you. In the future I suggest you use other means to prevent this from happening like . . ."

So, never allow yourself to be a judge in an altercation by students if you did not see who started it.

Providing Students with a Level System Approach to Shape Behavior

Purpose

The purpose of this issue is to teach your students to choose positive behaviors that will lead to classroom privileges.

Examples

John has been made aware by his teacher that certain behaviors will allow him classroom privileges while negative behaviors will prevent him from having classroom options. John has been clearly informed that in order to get extra time with the computer he must be able to sit in his seat for a specified period of time during a lesson. Once this behavior is successfully accomplished for a certain period of time John will have his right to use the computer during free periods of the day. However, John will also learn that negative behaviors will cause him to be denied such fun activities. It is hoped that John will learn to shape his behavior so that he receives positive rewards.

Mary is in a classroom where everyone starts out with privileges and can only lose them by acting inappropriately according to the teacher's standards. As long as Mary maintains positive classroom behavior she will enjoy privileges.

What May Not Work

When it comes to shaping behavior, teachers who wait until the behavior has occurred to develop rules are not helping the student determine or shape the outcome of their own behavior. A classroom where rules are not clear, or not posted, or where rewards and consequences are not clear creates a difficult environment for students who have a difficult time monitoring their own behavior. Hoping for internal controls on the parts of some children can be a costly mistake. While not all children may need external boundaries of rewards and consequences, it is not a bad idea to begin this process from the beginning of the school year since society works in the same manner. In society, following laws and rules provides positive outcomes while negative behavior choices can lead to serious social and legal difficulties.

Try This

With this system you have two possible choices. The first choice is called the Privileges for All Concept. With this concept all students start off the year with classroom privileges and are told they have them until they give you a reason to take it away. However, the reasons to lose privileges have to be posted (i.e., running in the halls). In this way, everyone has a vested interest in maintaining positive behavior.

The second option is called the Point and Level System. With this concept of shaping behavior all students begin at Level I and have the option of moving to Level II and then Level III. All levels are defined with both privileges and behaviors that must be maintained in order to stay at that level and behaviors that need to be accomplished to move to the next level. All behaviors have a point value and the teacher sets point goals to move to the next level. The behaviors listed can be designed to fit your class and the needs of the children.

According to Special Connections (2009) point and level systems are a behavioral management approach that have been commonly recommended by educators, used in programs for students that exhibit challenging behavior, and discussed in the literature. They are designed to be an organizational framework for managing student behavior where "students access greater independences and more privileges as they demonstrate increased behavioral control" (Heward, p. 306, 2012). Students learn appropriate behavior through clearly defined behavioral expectations and rewards, privileges, and consequences linked to those expectations. There are specific criteria for advancement to the next level where the student(s) enjoy more desirable contingencies. It is intended that students who proceed through the levels are more able to self-manage, capable of handling more responsibility and therefore enjoy greater independence. There are four main goals of point and level systems: (1) increasing appropriate behavior; (2) promoting academic achievement; (3) fostering a student's improvement through self-management; and (4) developing personal responsibility for social, emotional, and academic performance (Farrell, Smith, & Brownell, 1998).

Developing Manageable Consequences

Purpose

The purpose of this issue is to provide you with manageable and realistic guidelines for inappropriate behavior on the part of your students.

Examples

John is a student who has been giving Mrs. Green a difficult time all day. John now does something minimal but because Mrs. Green has not dealt with him all day she comes across very harshly with her consequences. John does not understand because he does not see the incident as serious. The consequence that Mrs. Green has given John is later realized by her as too harsh and as a result of feeling guilty lets him off the consequence early.

Mrs. Menendez has tried to ignore Julio's attention seeking behavior all day because that is what she was taught to do. However, she is now feeling that it is getting out of control and feels she has waited too long to address it. Because she feel inadequate and may have done the wrong thing she takes it out on Julio with a very harsh consequence that is totally unmanageable.

Mr. Longo has given William a consequence for an inappropriate behavior but William is a very manipulative young man. William cleans the garbage off the floor, straightens out the desks and books around the room all in sight of Mr. Longo. Mr. Longo then calls him up and says to him that he does not have to serve the consequence because of his cooperative behavior. William has learned how to manipulate the system.

What May Not Work

When it comes to providing consequences for inappropriate behavior, you must be very realistic, timely, and have the sense of conviction that the consequence you have chosen fits the behavior by the child. If this sense of equality between consequence and the type of inappropriate action is not met then you will be seen as over reactive, out of control, and your judgment will be questioned.

Because some teachers wait too long to address a behavior pattern their own frustration builds up and will sometime cloud the reality of the situation when they finally deal with it.

Try This

1. **Limits and Guidelines Are Very Necessary for a Child's Emotional Development.** For children, realistic, fair and well defined limits and guidelines represent a "safety net" within which they can behave. Children will know that any act of poor judgment will be brought to their attention if limits are well defined. Consequently, they will be brought back to the safety net. Being a teacher should not be a popularity contest. Such guidelines and limits should come from both the home and classroom. However, in some cases parents may not be equipped to provide the correct guidelines that make a child feel secure and therefore the school becomes the second chance for such options to be provided to the child.

2. **All Behavior Should Have a Consequence.** This means appropriate behavior is rewarded and negative behavior given consequences. Consistency, whether reward or consequence will assist the child in developing a frame of reference on how to behave.

3. **Consequences By Themselves Will Not Work.** Consequences tell children what not to do, but rewards tell children what behavior is acceptable. If long term changes in behavior are desired, then reward must be included. They can include verbal praise, written notes of thanks, extended playtime or computer time, or lunch with the teacher

4. **Consequences Should Be Limited To Something That You Can Control.** Quantity or severity of consequence is not always important. The most important thing to remember with discipline is that you begin it and you end it. Maintaining both boundaries is crucial. In too many situations, the teacher may begin the discipline but due to its harshness, unrealistic expectations of time, manipulation by children or inability of the teacher to follow through, there is no

closure. For young children with no concept of time, 2 minutes in a "time out" chair (controllable) rather than 10 minutes (uncontrollable) is just as productive. For older children it is very crucial to maintain realistic time limits since they can become more oppositional or defiant if the time is too long.

5. **Never Trade a Consequence For a Reward.** If children do something inappropriate and then something appropriate, then the two incidents should be treated separately. If you begin to trade off, children become confused and may be forced to become manipulative in order to get out of the consequence. You can complement the child for the good behavior and provide a reward but still explain that the inappropriate behavior consequence must still be carried out.

6. **Focus on Inappropriate Behavior, Not the Personality.** Remember, children are not stupid, their inappropriate behavior is unacceptable. You may want to use such phrases as poor judgment, inappropriate behavior, lapse of judgment, acting before thinking etc., when confronting the act. Focusing on the act allows children to save face. Children that tend to grow up in homes where personalities are attacked tend to model that behavior in their social relationships.

7. **Choose Your Battlegrounds Wisely.** Try to view energy like money. In this way, you will be deciding whether an issue is worth $2.00 worth of energy or $200.00. Investing too much energy in situations may lead to early teacher "burnout". However, it is very important that both teachers and assistant teachers agree on the priority of issues so that the child is not confused.

8. **Try to Project a United Front.** If one teacher should disagree with the other's tactics or reasoning, try to discuss it at a private moment. Open disagreement concerning a disciplinary action can sometimes confuse children and place them in the uncomfortable position of having to choose between teachers.

9. **Delay a Consequence When You Are Angry.** The use of delay allows for a different perspective than that which is viewed at the height of anger. Say, "I am so upset now so go to your seat and I'll deal with you in 15 minutes." The use of delay will reduce impractical consequences.

Removal of the Audience

Purpose

The purpose of this issue of the Classroom Management Series is to explain how not to allow yourself to get caught in a confrontation with a student who refuses to listen while in class.

Examples

Mrs. Janus is getting frustrated because Alasandro has been talking all day and is not getting her subtle looks or nonverbal indications to stop talking. She then asks him to please stop talking to his neighbor and the whole class turns to him to see what he is going to do. He responds that he is not and she can't make him. At this point Mrs. Janus is caught in a bind and could lose if she handles it incorrectly.

Mr. Stanos tells Maria to be quiet and pay attention. Matia, 14 years old with emotional disturbance does not want to look bad in front of her peers so she ignores him. Mr. Stanos get furious and threatens her with all sorts of repercussions but she still doesn't back down.

Mrs. Willow asks John politely to please try to not talk to the girl next to him. John hears her and wants to comply but doesn't want to look weak in front of the girl so he says, "What if I don't want to?" Mrs. Willow, despite her sensitivity is caught in a bind.

What May Not Work

What may not work in any of these cases is to confront the individual in front of the audience. Individuals with emotional problems have a very hard time backing down when caught in front of their peers. While many do not want to take it further, their weak self-esteem cannot offer them suitable ways of backing off. Caught by a sense of public humiliation, peer embarrassment versus teacher consequence, the individuals will usually opt for teacher consequence. Needless to say this can present a very dangerous position for a teacher. Individuals who have a weak self-esteem draw "strength" from an audience and have to play to that audience despite the serious consequences. What this can mean for a teacher is that the student will take it as far as possible without backing down.

Try This

Keeping in mind that the student draws "power" from the audience you have several options to consider:

- Step 1—You should always offer the student the option of settling him/herself down. However, the problem as well as the solution is all in your delivery. At first you can make a general statement to the class about the difficulty you have in doing your job when talking is going on. Pause and temporarily stare at the student after looking around the room. If that helps then the problem is solved. If not go to Step II.

- Step II—If the student continues approach his/her desk (See Proximity Teaching Tool) and teach the lesson right next to his/her desk. That will hopefully help. If that does not go to step III.
- Step III—Go your desk, take a minute and write a note suggesting that he/she cooperate and that you cannot allow him/her to continue doing this. Continue teaching and place the note on his/her desk. The privacy will allow the student to save face. If this does not work and the student is defiant go to step IV.
- Step IV—Go over to the desk and ask to speak with the student outside. If he/she follows then behind closed doors say, "I can no longer allow you to continue this behavior in class. If you choose to continue I will be forced to take action. I hope you do not choose to continue so I can do my job. Do you understand?" Hopefully that will work. However, the ultimate nightmare is in Step V.
- Step V—You might ask what happens if the student refuses to follow me outside? In that case ask the assistant to remove the class except for the student. Ask the aid to take the class into the hall and isolate the student. At that point follow Step IV. If he/she is still defiant you will have no choice but to get an administrator and let the student know that it is his/her decision not to follow the rules and his/her decision to receive the consequence. Never let them blame you for their opposition or defiance.

Dealing With Attention Seeking Students

Purpose

The purpose of this issue of the Classroom Management Series is to explain how to short circuit a student's need for inappropriate attention.

Examples

John is a student who gets very little attention or validation at home which has created feelings of insignificance and insecurity. As a result, he constantly seeks the attention of the teacher at inappropriate moments.

Mary is a girl who feels out of control, and as a result, needs to constantly be in control by clinging to the teacher during class time.

Jose is a boy who feels that if he is not noticed, he will feel alone and isolated. He feels unable to relate to his peers so he uses the teacher's time to "connect". However, the teacher has lost her patience with him because he doesn't listen.

What May Not Work

What may not work in these cases is to constantly "reject", reason or ignore the behaviors of these students. Since all behavior is a message, one must go beyond the behavior to try and understand what the student is trying to communicate. In these cases, as it will be in other similar cases, the student is seeking attention and recognition. While there is nothing wrong with these needs, it is the choice of fulfilling these needs that is creating the problem, not the needs themselves. As a result, the student is the one determining when he/she wants to have his/her needs met, which will often be at inappropriate times.

Try This

Since children who need attention will seek attention, the trick here is to change the control from the child to the teacher. In this way, the timing of the attention is in the hands of the teacher and can be done at appropriate times. What we suggest is that you go over to the child when he/she is not expecting attention as often as possible and either compliment, see how he/she is doing, make a positive observation, ask about something he/she mentioned that was going on in his/her life, or ask him/her to do a job for you. This consistent action should alleviate the need for seeking out attention at inappropriate times.

Be aware however, that the child may not believe you will continue to do this so it may take several attempts before they calm down and see that they are getting what they need without "asking inappropriately" for it.

Use Delay As a Discipline Tool

Purpose

The purpose of this Classroom Management Series is to allow you time to make better decisions about the outcomes of inappropriate behaviors.

Examples

Mrs. Carlos has had a very rough day with her students who are acting inappropriately in class. Besides that, she is under stress because of other issues in her private life. As a result her patience is wearing thin and her energy is low.

Ramon, a student in her class violates a serious rule. Mrs. Carlos yells at him and punishes him with a very involved consequence that is not realistic.

Mr. Edwards has had a very difficult night and is not feeling well. He has come to class today with many things on his mind. A child acts up and he quickly responds with a very punitive consequence that is a definite over-reaction to the incident.

What May Not Work

There is no doubt that teachers are human beings first and with that comes all the human frailties and issues that people struggle with on any given day. Consequently, these issues may be so draining that they pull away available energy from patience, a quality dependent on available energy. After all, the more energy we have, the more patience we have and vice-versa. What may not work in this situation is allowing yourself to not be aware of how drained you may be and how many issues you may be struggling with at this time. Believing that on these days you can handle things that may blind side you with good judgment is questionable.

Try This

Don't be afraid to delay a consequence when you are very angry. The use of delay allows for a different perspective than that viewed at the height of anger. There is nothing wrong with saying, "I am so angry right now that I don't want to deal with this situation. Go to your seat and I'll deal with you in 15 minutes." The use of delay will also reduce impractical consequences.

In conclusion, be aware that teaching is not a popularity contest but a responsibility. The opportunity to select from a variety of tools when confronted with a positive or negative situation can only enhance the difficult but rewarding job of teaching.

Find Alternate Methods to Spotlight Positive Behaviors or Skills

Purpose

The purpose of this tool is to systematically focus on a student's positive qualities.

Examples

Mr. Carson is angry at Carlos for making jokes during class which the class always finds funny. Mrs. Benson constantly has to tell Michael to stop drawing in his notebook during lessons. Mrs. Valdez has to refocus Janice back to the lesson because she is constantly writing stories or poems. Mr. Stanos finds it very hard to deal with Manuel's funny impressions of people at the wrong time.

What May Not Work

All of these students are exhibiting positive qualities that define them in some way but at the wrong time. If someone shows you beautiful photographs they have taken but does it during your wedding ceremony your focus is on the inappropriateness not the beauty. This also may happen in classrooms where students with special needs may not always act appropriately and many times positive aspects of their lives will be lost because of the poor timing of the act. Every student, has positive qualities and strengths that we must always look out for as teachers. While some student's make it difficult to see the positive because of the sheer frequency of inappropriate actions and behaviors, those positive traits are there none-the-less. If we miss them, we miss an extraordinary opportunity to help build a child's self-worth. Finding a positive skill or quality that a child can use to form a more positive identity is crucial.

Try This

What you will need to do from the very first day is interview the students or hand out questionnaires that can detect skills that they find interesting or qualities that they possess that will add to a feeling of self-worth or fulfillment. You will also need to find alternate ways of allowing these children to express their skills. You may want to hold a magic, talent and comedy session at the end of the school day for anyone who wishes to show off some talents. You may have poetry, photography, writing or drawing contests once a month to bring out the talents of others. Trying to squelch talent and positive skills will only frustrate the child more. Being in control of finding positive outlets will provide both you and the students with a positive feeling of validation.

Initiating Compliments

Purpose

The purpose of this technique is to avert negative behaviors that students exhibit for attention.

Examples

John calls out for the teacher's attention during a lesson and gets attention even though it is negative. Mary teases the student next to her and looks to see if the teacher is watching her because she needs to feel noticed. Mario wants to be noticed by the teacher so shows off at inappropriate times and is very silly.

What May Not Work

What may not work is trying to stop the need for attention through threats or serious disciplinary actions. This would be like trying to stop someone's hunger and need for food by threats. The asking may be temporarily contained but the need will eventually come out again, and may show with even more intensity.

Try This

To avoid students seeking out attention on their terms which may be in inappropriate and negative ways, go over to them as often as realistically possible and compliment them or engage them in some conversation. Going over and complimenting or making them feel important by using spontaneous actions should reduce their need to try to gain your attention negatively. Also, you will want to quickly reinforce positive behaviors. However, try to focus on ones that are observed by you that you can spontaneously respond to so that the student feels you noticed the behavior even though there was no intention on his/her part to do so.

What may also work here is to teach these students how to ask for attention in healthy ways. What you will need to teach them is to ask you

"When will you have time to speak with me," since you can provide this because you will determine a time that is right for both of you. Empowering students to ask for attention or reassurance is very healthy since they will get their needs fulfilled.

If a student cannot set his/her own boundaries and asks for this several times you will need to set a limit for the day and explain that you have to share your time with everyone but that he/she is important so use your request wisely.

Empowering children with options to ask for attention when they want, even if its limited, usually reduces their need for attention since they can get it anytime they want. Power is not having to use it, it is just the knowledge that you have it.

Drop Off

Purpose

The purpose of this technique is to avert impulsive inappropriate decisions on the part of the student.

Examples

You need to tell Jose that he will have to be responsible for finishing his classwork assignment which you understand was difficult so you adapted it for him. However, in order to teach him the sense of completion he must finish the adapted assignment. Jose is prone to over-reactions and blowing things out of proportion.

What May Not Work

What may not work in this case is calling Jose over and telling him directly that he will be responsible for finishing the classwork assignment during free time. Direct notification for reactive students only causes them to use the fragile skills of deflection (see fragile ego section) which occur without thinking and to avoid feeling inadequate or a failure. What Jose hears if you are direct is that you are a failure, cannot do what the others can do, and lack ability. Even though you never implied this a fragile ego always distorts what is being said because that is what Jose actually feels about himself.

Try This

With students like Jose use what we call a "drop off approach." A drop off approach in this case may go like this:

Jose before I give you this note I want to make it clear that I know you are trying very hard. I have seen many great things from you like _____ and _____. I know school is difficult at times but it is my job to help you succeed. Therefore, I want you to go to your seat and read my note. We can talk about it in 10 minutes. Do you understand?"

The note may say something like this:

Dear Jose,

I realized that the class assignment we did this morning was difficult for some students. There are several things I can do as a teacher to make it more understanding and easier for all of you to finish. I did just that and have attached the part that you need to finish. I want you to think carefully about this since finishing it now will make you feel much better about yourself and help you understand what you need to do the next time. The only time I can have you do this in our schedule is when we have free time. However, if you choose to finish it the way I have indicated, then I will arrange for you to have some personal free time this week. I hope you make the right decision since it must be completed.

Sincerely yours,

Mrs. _____

The "Drop Off" technique allows the more rational side of Jose to come forward since we are allowing him time to consider alternative. Presenting it directly will only be met by the impulse reactive side.

How to Help Students Feel Good About Themselves in Order to Reduce Inappropriate Behavior

14

Helping Students Feel Good About Themselves

Confident children seem to share certain characteristics. In their relationships with both teachers and parents, they show in many ways that they are empowered, hopeful, autonomous, resilient, and secure. They are also accomplished, receive recognition for their accomplishments, and persevere even when things don't go as they would like. Finally, for the most part they genuinely seem to enjoy life, both at school and at home. The ideas described here, if practiced in the classroom, will help students enjoy the environment they are in and believe in themselves as they never have before. The building of confidence in your students should be a process rather than a hit and miss approach. The following suggestions will enhance the factors in the human condition that lead to a sense of self-worth and overall confidence. Further, improving self-esteem will greatly reduce the need for tension related behavior patterns.

Remember, confidence is based on actual successful experiences, not just telling a student that he or she is intelligent, creative etc. so providing

The Classroom Teacher's Behavior Management Toolbox, pages 69–76

these opportunities will be crucial. The main goals in building confidence are to provide tasks and an environment that results in sense of completion and a sense of accomplishment.

1 Empowerment

Empowerment means being given the authority or power to act as you wish. For many students, knowing they are empowered is actually more important than actually exercising that power. In the classroom, the empowerment that comes from having educational tools they can turn to promotes a sense of security and helps build the foundation of confidence. Without a sense of empowerment, students may become rigid and hesitant, always waiting for you to tell them what to do next or how to solve problems.

Children who do not feel empowered:

- May be unwilling to try new things
- Hesitate initiating activities
- Procrastinate or use avoidance out of fear of asking questions
- Lack resources to solve problems
- Do not have the ability to see solutions
- Exhibit learned helplessness

Classroom Practices to enhance empowerment allow:

- Math tables and formulas during tests
- Calculators to check work
- Computer resources to find answers
- Dictionaries for in class writing assignments and spelling
- A thesaurus to help find words for writing assignments
- Giving several examples similar to upcoming problems or questions
- Permitting students to collaborate on finding answers
- Providing several alternate ways of responding to a task

2 Hope

Hope is desire accompanied by the belief in one's ability to complete of a task. When students feel hopeless, they feel powerless. If they have hope and believe they can succeed, students will tend to take more risks and chances.

Students who feel hopeless:

- Tend to give up easily

- Tend to negate his or her progress or ability
- Are unwilling to try things or take a chance
- Are resistant
- Are external in their thinking and believe, "why bother it really doesn't matter anyway"

Classroom Practices to foster hope

- Provide shorter but more frequent assignments to increase chances of completion and success.
- Check small groups of problems at a time rather than waiting until the end so that students can correct any mistakes they are making in the process prior to completing the entire task.
- Prove students with short, positive daily progress reports.
- Send parents reports on progress areas rather than problem areas. Word problem areas as "areas being worked on" or "areas in need of further attention." The language of a letter or note home can have positive or negative results and in turn affect the hope and motivation of the student to continue trying.
- Bridge areas that may give students trouble so that they can move on and complete the task. Teach them to ask for a "helping bridge" from you if they are stuck and not sure how to proceed.

3 Autonomy

Another important quality found in confident children is a sense of autonomy, or the belief that you have the ability to govern yourself. Individuals seek a quality of human functioning that has at its core the desire to determine their own behavior; they have an innate need to feel autonomous and to have control over their lives. "This need for self-determination is satisfied when individuals are free to behave of their own volition—to engage in activities because they want to, not because they have to. At its core is the freedom to choose and to have choices, rather than being forced or coerced to behave according to the desires of another" (James P Raffini, 1996; Shaffer, 2015, *150 Ways to Increase Intrinsic Motivation in the Classroom*).

Compared to students of controlling teachers and to pawn-like students, students of autonomy-supportive teachers and origin-like students show the following positive educational and developmental outcomes:

- Higher academic achievement
- Greater perceived competence

- Higher sense of self-worth and self-esteem
- Enhanced conceptual learning
- Greater creativity
- Preference for challenge
- More positive emotional tone
- Increased school attendance and retention

Deadlines, threats, competition, imposed goals, surveillance, and evaluations were all found to undermine intrinsic motivation. . . . It seemed that if controlling people—that is, pressuring them to behave in particular ways— diminishes their feelings of self-determination, then giving them choices about how to behave ought to enhance them. . . . Research has confirmed that choice enhances people's intrinsic motivation, so when people participate in decisions about what to do, they will be more motivated and committed to the task—to being sure that the task gets done well. . . . People who were asked to do a particular task but allowed the freedom of having some say in how to do it were more fully engaged by the activity—they enjoyed it more—than people who were not treated as unique individuals. . . . It is thus important that people in positions of authority begin to consider how to provide more choice. . . . Why not give students choice about what field trips to take and what topics to write their papers about, for example. (Edward Deci)

Why We Do What We Do

Students who lack autonomy will:

- Be more dependent
- Have problems offering opinions
- Be easily influenced by others
- Change their opinion if it is unpopular even if it is right
- Lack direction or a plan of action

Classroom Practices to Enhance Autonomy

- Give students time to do independent work, enjoy hobbies, or pursue areas of interest and curiosity
- Allow students to work on their own ideas
- Allow students choices or options for projects rather than telling them what must be done
- Allow students to share their own ideas and areas of interests with others

- Give students responsibility for aspects of their own learning (i.e., determining the order of lessons, types of evaluation measures used, timelines for completion)

4 Resiliency

Resiliency is the ability to bounce back from unsuccessful experiences and maintain a perspective that requires the student to think about what needs to be done to change the outcome the next time. A student with high resiliency who fails a test is likely to be willing to look at the factors that contributed to his lack of success, then try again. Resiliency is an important component of self-confidence and success.

Students who lack resiliency:

- Give up easily
- Have low frustration tolerances
- Pout
- Become stubborn and withdrawn when confronted with frustration
- See everything as negative
- Become blame oriented
- Become self-deprecating

Classroom Practices to Enhance Resiliency

- Provide repeated successful experiences even if the task or job being given was given and successfully completed several times before
- Provide students with the opportunity to correct their work to master concepts and improve their grades
- Give students the opportunity to drop their lowest grade so that one bad score does not destroy his/her motivation
- Teach the child to set realistic attainable goals

5 Accomplishment

A feeling of accomplishment is the sense that you have brought something about by your own efforts. Confidence is the belief that one's behavior will, for the most part, lead to successful completion of tasks or projects. In Positive Restructuring this sense of accomplishment is enhanced by assigning work that will ensure student's success.

Feeling a sense of accomplishment does not mean that a task or assignment must be completed in its entirety. A child can feel good about him or herself because he/she was able to find a specific answer to part of an assignment, persevered in his/her work, or gave it his/her best effort.

A sense of accomplishment provides closure, a necessary factor in believing in one's ability and one's capacity to be successful.

Children who lack a sense of accomplishment will:

- Procrastinate
- Avoid
- Give up very easily on a task
- See every task as too hard

Classroom Practices to Enhance a Sense of Accomplishment

- Have parents check homework every night so that all assignment are complete when the child comes to school
- Provide tasks, in whatever form possible, that allow for the highest chance of accomplishment and closure
- Provide assignments, projects, and tasks in such a way as to control successful outcomes
- Have students use a step by step approach to tasks and assignments so that they can feel successful at the completion of every step
- Provide sufficient time for students to complete work or extra time for students who need it. Remember a sense of accomplishment is the key
- Give students a checklist of work they have completed rather than lists of work they need to complete.

6 Recognition

Everyone needs to be recognized—to receive special notice or attention. Parents normally provide much of a child's need for recognition. However, teachers are a very close second to parents when it comes to a child's desire to please and be recognized for performance and effort. Without recognition, students may lose their desire to try, believing that no one cares what they do. Recognition enhances motivation, especially intrinsic motivation—that is, choosing to do an activity not for external rewards but for the internal satisfaction derived from the activity itself. Although recognition is an extrinsic or external reward, over time it becomes internalized.

Children who do not feel a sense of recognition will:

- Crave attention at inappropriate times
- Use spotlight behaviors (i.e., class clown) to derive negative recognition
- May exhibit frequent visits to the nurse
- Put down other students who are getting recognition in positive ways
- Find negative ways to gain recognition (i.e., bully)

Classroom Practices That Enhance a Feeling of Recognition

- Provide frequent verbal or written validation (e.g., "Thanks for helping Billy yesterday, Good job in keeping your desk neat)
- Give spontaneous notes of praise and leave them on the student's desk
- Write positive notes and letters to parents
- Go to students with complements rather than them always feeling they have to do something to get recognition
- Share a student's success outside of school with the class
- Have a positive recognition day where everyone gets to share nice things they have done

7 Perseverance

Perseverance means to pursue a goal in the face of difficulty, discouragement, frustration, or opposition. Continuing when the going is rough means that students have built enough confidence to have internalized the belief that there is a direct relationship between effort and achievement. Once students have internalized this belief, they are less frustrated and more resilient, solution oriented, willing to take chances and be goal oriented.

Children who lack perseverance will:

- Give up easily
- Throw tantrums or pout when frustrated
- Verbally beat themselves up
- Be resistant to new activities

Classroom Practices to Enhance Perseverance

- Provide rewards for trying
- Recognize sustained effort

- Break down long term assignments into manageable steps
- Have students work in teams to have a sense of group accomplishment and help each other through hard times
- Give rewards at several steps along the way to enhance the desire to stick with something to the end

In conclusion, you have the power to provide a wonderful environment where children can grow, learn, and most of all feel great about themselves and their ability. Confidence does not happen by chance, and your role, especially in today's society is so very crucial in determining the outcome of a child's self-worth and feelings about his/her future.

SECTION **VI**

Final Word

15

Final Points

Let recap the main points to keep in mind when working with children in the classroom. These issues are crucial if you are going to create a safe environment for everyone and one with very clear fair boundaries within which children can learn and prosper.

1. **Limits and Guidelines Are Very Necessary for a Child's Emotional Development.** For children, realistic, fair, and well defined limits and guidelines represent a "safety net" within which they can behave. Children will know that any act of poor judgment will be brought to their attention if limits are well defined. Consequently, they will be brought back to the safety net. Setting boundaries and creating rewards and consequences for inappropriate behavior can never be a popularity contest.

2. **All Behavior Should Have a Consequence.** This means appropriate behavior is rewarded and negative behavior punished. Consistency of consequence, whether reward or punishment will assist the child in developing a frame of reference on how to behave.

The Classroom Teacher's Behavior Management Toolbox, pages 79–81

3. **Discipline by Itself Will Not Work.** Punishment tells children what not to do, but rewards tell children what behavior is acceptable. If long term changes in behavior are desired, then reward must be included. Rewards can include verbal praise, written notes of thanks, extended free time or computer time, special trip or lunch with the teacher.

4. **Punishment Should Be Limited to Something That You Can Control.** Quantity or severity of punishment is not always important. The most important thing to remember with discipline is that a teacher begins it and the teacher ends it. Maintaining both boundaries is crucial. In some situations a teacher may begin the discipline but due to its harshness, unrealistic expectations of time manipulation by children or inability of the teacher to follow through, there is no closure. For young children with no concept of time, two minutes in a "time out" chair (controllable) rather than 30 minutes (uncontrollable) is just as productive.

5. **Never Trade a Punishment for a Reward.** If children do something inappropriate and then something appropriate, then the two incidents should be treated separately. If you begin to trade off, children become confused and may be forced to become manipulative.

6. **Focus on Inappropriate Behavior, Not the Personality.** Remember, children are not stupid, their inappropriate behavior is unacceptable. You may want to use such phrases as poor judgment, inappropriate behavior, lapse of judgment, acting before thinking etc., when confronting the act. Focusing on the act allows children to save face. Children that tend to grow up in homes where personalities are attacked tend to model that behavior in their social relationships.

7. **Choose Your Battlegrounds Wisely.** Try to view energy like money. In this way, you will be deciding whether an issue is worth $2.00 worth of energy or $200.00. Investing too much energy in situations may lead to early teacher "burnout". However, it is very important that both the teacher and the assistant teacher agree on the priority of issues so that the child is not confused.

8. **Try to Use a Forced Choice Technique Whenever Possible.** Choose two options, solutions, and alternatives etc. that are acceptable to you. Then say to the child, "You may do... or... Which do you prefer"? Using a forced choice technique allows children to feel that they are making the decision and creates less problems than an open ended question such as, "What would you like?"

9. **Delay a Consequence When You Are Angry.** The use of delay allows for a different perspective than that which is viewed at the height

of anger. Say, "I am so angry now that I don't want to deal with this situation. Go to your seat and I'll deal with you in 15 minutes." The use of delay will reduce impractical consequences.

References

Farrell, D. T., Smith, S. W., & Brownell, M. T. (1998). Teacher perceptions of level system effectiveness on the behavior of students with emotional or behavioral disorders. *The Journal of Special Education, 32*(2), 89–98.

Heward, W. L. (2012). *Exceptional children: An introduction to special education* (10th ed.). Upper Saddle River, NJ: Pearson Education, Inc.

Raffini, J. P. (1995) *150 ways to increase intrinsic motivation in the classroom.* Upper Saddle River, NJ: Pearson Education, Inc.

Shaffer, S. C. (2015). *Motivation and personal autonomy.* Retrieved on September 230, 2015 from: http://www2.yk.psu.edu/sites/scs15/teaching-learning-resources2/teaching-learning-topics-resources/motivation/

Suggested Readings

Alberto, P. A., & Troutman, A. C. (2006). *Applied behavior analysis for teachers* (7th ed.). Upper Saddle River, NJ: Pearson.

Alderman, T. W. (1991). *The discipline a total approach resource book: Classroom discipline's "greatest hits."* Beaufort, SC: Author.

Alderman, T. (2000). *Classroom discipline: The effective use of negative consequences.* Beaufort, SC: Resources for Professionals.

American Psychological Association Zero Tolerance Task Force. (2008). Are zero tolerance policies effective in the schools? An evidentiary review and recommendations. *American Psychologist, 63*, 852–862.

Baer, G. G. (2015). Preventative classroom strategies. In E. T. Emmer & E. J. Sabornie (Eds.), *Handbook of classroom management* (2nd ed.) (pp. 15–39). New York, NY: Taylor & Francis Group.

The Classroom Teacher's Behavior Management Toolbox, pages 83–88
Copyright © 2016 by Information Age Publishing

Bender, W. W., & Mathes, M. Y. (1995). Students with ADHD in inclusive classrooms: A hierarchical approach to strategy selection. *Intervention in School and Clinic, 30*, 226–234.

Bjorklund, D. (2005). *Children's thinking: Cognitive development and individual differences.* Belmont, CA: Wadsworth/Thomson Learning. Hawthorn Educational Services, Inc.

Bluestein, J. (2001). *Creating emotionally safe schools: A guide for educators and parents.* Deerfield Beach, FL: Health Communications, Inc.

Boniecki, K. A., & Moore, S. (2003). Breaking the silence: Using a token economy to reinforce classroom participation. *Teaching of Psychology, 30*, 224–227.

Bradshaw, C. (2014) Positive behavioral interventions and supports. In Slavin, R. E. (Ed.), *Classroom management and assessment* (pp. 99–104). Thousand Oaks, CA: Corwin.

Brady, K., Forton, M. B., Porter, D., & Wood, C. (2003). *Rules in school.* Turners Falls, MA: Northeast Foundation for Children, Inc.

Brophy, J. (2006). History of research on classroom management. In C. M. Evertson & C. S. Weinstein (Eds.), *Handbook of classroom management: Research, practice, and contemporary issues* (pp. 17–43). Mahwah, NJ: Erlbaum.

Buisson, G. J., Murdock, J. Y., & Reynolds, K. E. (1995). Effects of tokens on response latency of students with hearing impairments in a resource room. *Education and Treatment of Children, 18*(4), 408–421.

Burke, J. (2008). *Classroom management.* New York, NY: Scholastic, Inc.

Canter, L. (2010). *Lee Canter's assertive discipline: Positive behavior management for today's classroom.* Bloomington, IN: Solution Tree, Inc.

Carpenter, L. B. (2001). Utilizing travel cards to increase productive student behavior, teacher collaboration, and parent-school communication. *Education and Training in Mental Retardation and Developmental Disabilities, 36*(3), 318–322.

Cavalier, A. R., Ferretti, R. P., & Hodges, A. F. (1997). Self-management within a classroom token economy for students with learning disabilities. *Research in Developmental Disabilities, 18*(3), 167–178.

Cooper, J. O. (1987). Token economy. In J. O. Cooper, T. E. Heron, & W. L. Heward (Eds.), *Applied behavior analysis.* Columbus, OH: Merrill.

Crone, D. H., & Horner, R. H. (2003). *Building positive behavior support systems in schools: Functional behavioral assessment.* New York, NY: Guilford.

Crone, D. H., Horner, R. H., & Hawken, L. S. (2004). *Responding to behavior problems in schools: The behavior education program.* New York, NY: Guilford.

Cummings, C. (2001) *Managing to teach: A guide to classroom management.* Edmonds, WA: Teaching, Inc.

Curwin, R. L., & Mendler, A. N. (2008). *Discipline with dignity.* Alexandria, VA: Association for Supervision and Curriculum Development.

Cushman, K., & Rogers, L. (2008). *Fires in the bathroom: Advice for teachers from middle schoolers.* New York, NY: The New Press. Note: A separate book is written from the high school perspective.

DeBruyn, R. L., & Larson, J. L. (1992). *You can handle them all quick-action card deck.* Manhattan, KS: The Master Teacher, Inc. Note: The cards are cheaper, but the book that goes with this has been updated as of 2008.

Denton, P. (2007) *The power of our words: Teacher language that helps children learn.* Turners Falls, MA: Northeast Foundation for Children, Inc.

Durlak, J. A., Weissberg, R. P., Dymnicki, A. B., Taylor, R. D., & Schellinger, K. B. (2011). The impact of enhancing students' social and emotional learning: A meta-analysis of school-based universal interventions. *Child Development, 82,* 405–432.

Emmer, E. T., & Sabornie, E. J. (Eds.). (2015). *Handbook of classroom management* (2nd ed.). New York, NY: Routledge.

Emmer, E. T., & Evertson, C. M. (2009). *Classroom management for middle and high school teachers.* Upper Saddle River, NJ: Pearson.

Emmer, E., Evertson, C. M., & Anderson, L. (1980). Effective management at the beginning of the school year. *Elementary School Journal, 80,* 219–231.

Evertson, C. M., & Weinstein, C. S. (2006). Classroom management as a field of inquiry. In C. M. Evertson & C. S. Weinstein (Eds.), *Handbook of classroom management: Research, practice, and contemporary issues* (pp. 3–16). Mahwah, NJ: Erlbaum.

Evertson, C. M., & Emmer, E. (1982). Effective management at the beginning of the year in junior high school classrooms. *Journal of Educational Psychology, 74,* 485–498.

Filcheck, H. A., McNeil, C. B., Greco, L. A., & Bernard, R. S. (2004). Using a whole-class token economy and coaching of teacher skills in a preschool classroom to manage disruptive behavior. *Psychology in the Schools, 4*(3), 351–361.

Freiberg, H. J., & Lapointe, J. M. (2006). Research-based programs for preventing and solving discipline problems. In C. M. Evertson and C. S. Weinstein (Eds.). *Handbook of classroom management: Research, practice, and contemporary issues* (pp. 735–786). Mahwah, NJ: Lawrence Erlbaum Associates.

Glasser, W. (2008). *Every student can succeed.* Chatsworth, CA: William Glasser, Inc.

Haggart, W. (2009). *Discipline and learning styles: An educator's guide.* Cadiz, KY: Performance Learning Systems, Inc.

Harlan, J. C., & Rowland, S. T. (2002). *Behavior management strategies for teachers: Achieving instructional effectiveness, student success, and student motivation—Every teacher and any student can!* Springfield, IL: Charles C. Thomas Publisher, Ltd.

Higgins, J. W., Williams, R. L., & McLaughlin, T. F. (2001). The effects of a token economy employing instructional consequences for a third-grade student with learning disabilities: A data-based case study. *Education and Treatment of Children, 42*(1), 99–106.

Hubb, S. D. A., & Reitman, D. (1999). Improving sports skills and sportsmanship in children diagnosed with attention-deficit/hyperactivity disorder. *Child and Family Behavior Therapy, 21*(3), 35–51.

Huitt, W. (2004). *Maslow's hierarchy of needs. Educational Psychology Interactive.* Valdosta, GA: Valdosta State University. Retrieved April 22, 2009 from http://chiron.valdosta.edu/whuitt/col/regsys/maslow.html.

Jensen, E. (2009). *Teaching with poverty in mind: What being poor does to kids' brains and what schools can do about it.* Alexandria, VA: Association for Supervision and Curriculum Development.

Johnston, B. D. (1995). "Withitness": Real or fictional? *The Physical Educator, 52*(1), 22–28.

Jones, F. H., Jones, P., & Jones, J. L. (2007). *Tools for teaching: discipline, instruction, motivation* (2nd ed.). Santa Cruz, CA: F.H. Jones & Associates.

Kahng, S. W., Boscoe, J. H., & Byrne, S. (2003). The use of escape contingency and a token economy to increase food acceptance. *Journal of Applied Behavior Analysis, 36,* 349–353.

Kern, L., & Clemens, N. H. (2007). Antecedent strategies to promote appropriate classroom behavior. *Psychology in the Schools, 44,* 65–75.

Kottler, J. A. (2002). *Students who drive you crazy: Succeeding with resistant, unmotivated, and otherwise difficult young people.* Thousand Oaks, CA: Corwin Press.

Kounin, J. (1970). *Discipline and group management in classrooms.* New York, NY: Holt, Rinehart, & Winston.

Lannie, A. L., & Martens, B. K. (2004). Effects of task difficulty and type of contingency on students' allocation of responding to math worksheets. *Journal of Applied Behavior Analysis, 37,* 53–65.

Levin, J., & Nolan, J. F. (2003). *What every teacher should know about classroom management.* Boston, MA: Pearson Education, Inc.

Lewis, T. J., Mitchell, B. S., Trussell, R., & Newcommer, L. (2015). In E. T. Emmer & E. J. Sabornie (Eds.), *Handbook of classroom management* (2nd ed.) (pp. 40–59). New York, NY: Taylor & Francis Group.

Lindberg, J. A., Kellye, D. E., & Swick, A. S. (2005). *Common-sense classroom management for middle and high school teachers.* Thousand Oaks, CA: Corwin Press.

MacKenzie, R. J. (2003). *Setting limits in the classroom: How to move beyond the dance of discipline in today's classrooms.* New York, NY: Three Rivers Press.

Marzano, R. J., Gaddy, B. B., Foseid, M. C. Foseid, M. P., & Marzano, J. S. (2003). *A handbook for classroom management that works.* Alexandria, VA: Association for Supervision and Curriculum Development.

Marzano, R. J., Marzano, J. S., & Pickering, D. J. (2003). *Classroom management that works: Research-based strategies for every teacher.* Alexandria, VA: Association for Supervision and Curriculum Development.

McCarney, S. & Wunderlich, K. (2006). *Pre-referral intervention manual.* Columbia, MO: Hawthorne Educational Services, Inc.

McLeod, J., Fisher, J., & Hoover, G. (2003). *The key elements of classroom management: Managing time and space, student behavior, and instructional strategies.* Alexandria, VA: Association for Supervision and Curriculum Development.

Mendler, A. N. (2001). *Connecting with students.* Alexandria, VA: Association for Supervision and Curriculum Development.

Mendler, A. N. (2012). *When teaching gets tough: Smart ways to reclaim your game.* Alexandria, VA: Association for Supervision and Curriculum Development.

Moore, J. W., Tingstrom, D. H., Doggett, R. A., & Carlyon, W. D. (2001). Restructuring an existing token economy in a psychiatric facility for children. *Child and Family Behavior Therapy, 23*(3), 51–57.

Ridnouer, K. (2006). *Managing your classroom with heart: A guide for nurturing adolescent learners.* Alexandria, VA: Association for Supervision and Curriculum Development.

Quinn, P. (2009). *Ultimate RTI: Everything a teacher needs to know to implement RTI.* Singer, WI: Ideas Unlimited Seminars, Inc.

Robinson, S. L., & Griesemer, S. M. R. (2006). Helping individual students with problem behavior. In C. M. Evertson & C. S. Weinstein (Eds.), *Handbook of classroom management: Research, practice, and contemporary issues* (pp. 787–802). Mahwah, NJ: Erlbaum.

Rothstein-Fisch, C., & Trumbull, E. (2008). *Managing diverse classrooms: How to build on students' cultural strengths.* Alexandria, VA: Association for Supervision and Curriculum Development.

Savage, T. V. (1999). *Teaching self-control through management and discipline* (2nd ed.). Needham Heights, MA: Allyn & Bacon.

Savage, T. V., & Savage, M. K. (2010). *Successful classroom management and discipline: Teaching self-control and responsibility* (3rd ed.). Los Angeles, CA: Sage.

Scott, T. M., McIntyre, J., Liaupsin, C., Nelson, C. M., Conroy, M., & Payne, L. D. (2005). An examination of the relation between functional behavior assessment and selected intervention strategies with school-based teams. *Journal of Positive Behavior Interventions, 7,* 205–215.

Shellard, E., Protheroe, N., & Turner, J. (2005). *What we know about: Effective classroom management to support student learning.* Arlington, VA: Educational Research Service.

Slavin, R. E. (Ed.). (2014). *Classroom management & assessment.* Thousand Oaks, CA: Corwin Press.

Smith, R. (2004). *Conscious classroom management: Unlocking the secrets of great teaching.* San Rafael, CA: Conscious Teaching Publications.

Sugai, G., & Simonsen, B. (2015). Supporting general classroom management: Tier 2/3 practices and systems. In E. T. Emmer & E. J. Sabornie (Eds.), *Handbook of classroom management* (2nd ed.). New York, NY: Taylor & Francis Group.

Truchlicka, M., McLaughlin, T. F., & Swain, J. C. (1998). Effects of token reinforcement and response cost on the accuracy of spelling performance with middle-school special education students with behavior disorders. *Behavioral Interventions, 13,* 1–10.

Walker, J. R. (2012). *Interventions that work with high school students.* Atlanta, GA: Jordan Reeves Associates, Inc.

Weissberg, R. P., Kumpfer, K. L., & Seligman, M. E. P. (2003). Prevention that works for children and youth: An introduction. *American Psychologist, 58,* 425–432.

Whyte, D. (2008). *You can't teach a class you can't manage.* Peterborough, NJ: Crystal Springs Books.

About the Authors

Dr. Roger Pierangelo

Dr. Roger Pierangelo is a Full Professor in the Department of Special Education and Literacy at Long Island University. He has been an administrator of special education programs, served for 18 years as a permanent member of Committees on Special Education, has over 30 years of experience in the public school system as a general education classroom teacher and school psychologist, and a consultant to numerous private and public schools, PTA and SEPTA groups. Dr. Pierangelo has also been an evaluator for the New York State Office of Vocational and Rehabilitative Services, director of a private clinic and special education consultant to CNN News and US News and World Report. He is a New York State licensed clinical psychologist and has been in private practice for over 25 years, certified school psychologist, and a Board Certified Diplomate Fellow in Child and Adolescent Psychology and Forensic Psychology. Dr. Pierangelo currently holds the office of Executive Director of the National Association of Special Education Teachers (NASET), Executive Director of The American Academy of Special Education Professionals (**AASEP**), and Vice-President of The National Association of Parents with Children in Special Education (**NAPCSE**).

Dr. Pierangelo earned his BS from St. John's University, MS from Queens College, Professional Diploma from Queens College, PhD from Yeshiva University, and Diplomate Fellow in Child and Adolescent Psychology and Forensic Psychology from the International College of Professional Psychol-

The Classroom Teacher's Behavior Management Toolbox, pages 89–91
Copyright © 2016 by Information Age Publishing

ogy. Dr. Pierangelo is a member of the American Psychological Association, New York State Psychological Association, Nassau County Psychological Association, New York State Union of Teachers, and Phi Delta Kappa.

Dr. Pierangelo is the author of the *Special Educator's Survival Guide* and the *Special Education Teacher's Book of Lists*, published by Jossey Bass and author of *301 Ways to be a Loving Parent*, published by SPI Publishers. He is is the co-author of *The Educator's Diagnostic Manual of Disabilities and Disorders (EDM)*, *The Special Educators Comprehensive Guide to 301 Diagnostic Tests*, and *The Special Educator's Complete Guide to 109 Diagnostic Tests*, all published by Jossey Bass; the co-author of college textbooks titled, *Assessment in Special Education: A Practical Approach (4th ed.)*; *Transition Services in Special Education: A Practical Approach; and Learning Disabilities: A Practical Approach to Foundations, Diagnosis, Assessment, and Teaching*, all published by Allyn and Bacon; co-author of *Why Your Students Do What They Do—And What to Do When They Do It—Grades K–5; Why Your Students Do What They Do—And What to Do When They Do It—Grades 6–12; Creating Confident Children in the Classroom: The Use of Positive Restructuring*, and *What Every Teacher Should Know about Students with Special Needs*, all published by Research Press; co-author of *The Big Book of Special Education Resources*, and the co-author of an eight book *"The Educator's Step-by-Step Guide to . . ."* 10-book series, with the titles: *The Educator's Step-by-Step Guide to IEP Development, The Educator's Step-by-Step Guide to the 100 Most FAQ Asked by About Special Education the Special Education Process, The Educator's Step-by-Step Guide to Eligibility in Special Education, The Educator's Step-by-Step Guide to Assessment in Special Education, The Educator's Step-by-Step Guide to Working with Students with ADHD, The Educator's Step-by-Step Guide to Response to Intervention (RTI), The Educator's Step-by-Step Guide to Classroom Management for Students with Emotional and Behavioral Disorders, The Educator's Step-by-Step Guide to Setting Up Your Special Education Classroom, The Educator's Step-by-Step Guide to Classroom Management for Students with Autism, and The Educator's Step-by-Step Guide to Classroom Management for Students with Learning Disabilities.*

Dr. George Giuliani Jr.

Dr. George Giuliani is an Associate Professor at Hofstra University's School of Education and former Director of the Graduate School programs in Special Education. He is also an Adjunct Professor at Hofstra University's Maurice A Deane School of Law where he teaches the course, Special Education Law. Dr. Giuliani earned his BA from the College of the Holy Cross, MS from St. John's University, JD from City University of New York School of Law and MA and PsyD from Rutgers University. He earned Board Certification as a Diplomate Fellow in Advanced Child and Adolescent Psychology, Board Certification as a Diplomate Fellow in Forensic Sciences from the International College of Professional Psychology and Board Certification in Special Education from the American Academy of Special Education Professionals.

Dr. Giuliani is a member of the American Psychological Association, Education Law Association, New York State Psychological Association, American Bar Association, Suffolk County Psychological Association, Psi Chi, American Association of University Professors, and the Council for Exceptional Children. Dr. Giuliani is the Executive Director of The National Association of Special Education Teachers, Executive Director of the American Academy of Special Education Professionals, and President of the National Association of Parents with Children in Special Education. He has been a consultant for school districts and early childhood agencies, and has provided numerous workshops for parents, teachers and other professionals on a variety of special education and psychological topics.

Dr. Giuliani is the co-author of various articles in the *New York State Family Law Review* of the New York State Bar Association. He is the co-author of *The Educator's Diagnostic Manual of Disabilities and Disorders (EDM), The Special Educators Comprehensive Guide to 301 Diagnostic Tests*, and *The Special Educator's Complete Guide to 109 Diagnostic Tests*, all published by Jossey Bass; the co-author of college textbooks titled, *Assessment in Special Education: A Practical Approach (3rd ed.); Transition Services in Special Education: A Practical Approach; and Learning Disabilities: A Practical Approach to Foundations, Diagnosis, Assessment, and Teaching*, all published by Allyn and Bacon; co-author of *Why Your Students Do What They Do—And What to Do When They Do It—Grades K–5; Why Your Students Do What They Do—And What to Do When They Do It—Grades 6–12; Creating Confident Children in the Classroom: The Use of Positive Restructuring, and What Every Teacher Should Know about Students with Special Needs*, all published by Research Press; co-author of *The Big Book of Special Education Resources, Teaching Students With Learning Disabilities; Teaching in a Special Education Classroom; Teaching Students With Autism Spectrum Disorders; Classroom Management for Students With Emotional and Behavioral Disorders; Frequently Asked Questions About Response to Intervention; Classroom Management Techniques for Students With ADHD; Understanding Assessment in the Special Education Process; Understanding, Developing, and Writing Effective IEPs; Special Education Eligibility:* and *100 Frequently Asked Questions About the Special Education Process*, all published by Corwin Press.

Dr. Giuliani recently completed his latest book with Jessica Kingsley Publishers, *The Comprehensive Guide to Special Education Law.*